Wales
in cameracolour

PHOTOGRAPHS BY F. A. H. BLOEMENDAL

TEXT BY ALAN HOLLINGSWORTH

LONDON

IAN ALLAN LTD

First published 1978
Reprinted 1981

ISBN 0 7110 0802 7

Published by Ian Allan Ltd, Shepperton, Surrey;
and printed in Italy by
Graphische Betriebe Athesia, Bolzano

Introduction

The jewel that is Wales presents many facets to the outside world. To some it is the land of song — the Treorchy Male Voice choir and the Royal National Eisteddfod. To others it is the land of rugby football — hard-muscled packs from the hard-slogging mining valleys and the *hywl* at Twickenham and Cardiff Arms Park. To others still it is a land of poetry — not just the melodic cadence of the Welsh language but of English transformed and transcended — the Wales of Dylan Thomas' 'Do not go gentle into that good night' as much as the Wales of *Mor ddu a bol buwch* (as black as the inside of a cow). Whilst every visitor will catch his own brief glimpse of each of these facets — and many others too — it is the physical face of Wales, and the one we have sought to reflect in these pages, that will make its immediate and lasting impression. This is the Wales of mountain, lake and castle — often shrouded in mist, always shrouded in legend and mystery.

Geographically and historically, Wales *is* a castle. Though Shakespeare wrote of England, '. . . a fortress built by Nature for herself', the description is even more apt for Wales. Nature has given Wales a structure that resembles that of the many medieval castles with which the land abounds — moated outer ramparts, an inner and an outer ward, and a massive rugged keep to which the garrison can retreat when all else seems lost. And frequently through their turbulent history, the Welsh people have taken refuge in their mountain fastness and survived. With them and their Celtic imagination has survived too a wealth of folklore to make this already mysterious land a place of wonder and magic quite unique in the modern everyday world. Wales is not just a castle — it is a fairy castle.

The keep or inner bastion of the Welsh fastness lies in the old kingdom of Gwynedd — a name now taken for a modern administrative district — which used to cover the northern part of the country and was bounded by the sea on the north and west and to the south and east by the valleys of the Dee and the Dovey. In this area, rugged and forbidding over the centuries, lie the springs of Welsh culture and language and all the truly genuine mountains of Wales. It is as separate from the rest of Wales to the south of it as it is from England in the east. It is a veritable national redoubt that in days of old not only barred the way to the alien invader but also repelled the coloniser and the settler who might have followed in his wake. And even today when the tourists flood into the vast Snowdonia National Park in their thousands, the occupation is only seasonal. When the winter gales tear at the ancient rocks and heavy snow-laden clouds obscure the mountain tops, it remains the essentially Welsh heart of Wales.

It also, for the most part, speaks Welsh and though the visitor will only rarely find himself in a place or a situation where only Welsh is spoken — about 25 per cent of the population use Welsh as a first language and the majority of those are bi-lingual — some slight knowledge of Welsh and a Welsh dictionary add immeasurably to the pleasure of sight-seeing in Wales. The majority of Welsh place-names are not only descriptive, they are often accurately descriptive and much can be learned from them. For example, that place that even the Welsh abbreviate to Llanfair P.G. on the Anglesey shore of the Menai Strait — Llanfairpwllgwyngyllgogery-chwyrndrobwllllantysiliogogogoch can be translated as 'the church of St Mary by the hollow of the white aspen, over the whirlpool, and St Tysilio's Church close to the red cave'. Few Welsh place-names rival that for complexity, however, and even a few words (see p.15) can serve as a key to a fascinating treasure trove of geography, folk history and legend. Welsh has no distinctive script of its own and uses the same alphabet as English — a fact that makes the task of the Welsh language enthusiasts in altering road signs slightly easier. From their handiwork the visitor can also learn something of Welsh orthography because invariably both English and Welsh spelling can be seen. In Welsh *y* and *w* are vowels — *w* is pronounced like 'oo' in English; *y* variously as an 'ee' in words of one syllable, as an 'i' in others or as the 'u' in 'fur' in hyphenated words. The Welsh alphabet omits the consonants j, k, q, v, x, and z; has one 'f' pronounced 'v' and a double 'ff' which equals the English 'f'. It also has a 'dd' which is equivalent of 'th'. Far and away the most difficult for foreigners is the often-recurring double —

'll'. It is a sound that can be made by placing the tongue against the upper gums and breathing out – and has no English equivalent. Legend has it that when the Tower of Babel was destroyed and the builders were endowed with many tongues, the Welshman was gazing up at the tower dreaming of the mountains of his homeland when a large dollop of mortar landed in his mouth – '*ll*' was the noise he made expelling it! The fact is that Welsh is descended from the common Aryan stock that lies at the root of most European language. It belongs to a group known as 'P-Celt' along with Cornish and Breton which a Welsh speaker could understand. (Another group 'Q-Celt', Irish, Scots Gaelic and Manx a Welshman would not understand.) This distinction gives us a clue to the origins of the Welsh people themselves – not Welsh (the Anglo Saxons called them that – *Wealas,* foreigners) but Celtic.

The Celts were a warrior people who spread across Western Europe before the rise of the Roman Empire. They founded no lasting state and preferred a pastoral to an agricultural life. They were strong, formidable foes but they lacked discipline and Cato, the Roman statesman, described them as 'devoted to warfare and witty conversation'. Their religious leaders were the Druids, and in Wales the island of Anglesey became a great centre of Druidic lore. Not a great deal is known about what the Druids actually did or what they taught but poetry and song had their part as did the darker side of primitive religion in the practice of human sacrifice. These Celts were in occupation of the whole of the British Isles when the Romans began their conquest in AD 43. Inside four years they had subdued most of what we now call England. It took them more than 40 years to suppress the Celts of Cambria but thereafter they remained in occupation for 400 years. In that time the language of the local Celts underwent a change – just as it did in other Roman provinces. This process of change was hastened further in the confused period that attended the break-up of the Roman Empire. Celtic – now in the process of becoming 'Briton' – acquired a number of Latin words and phrases which remain to this day: *ffenestr* for window, *pont* for bridge. Since Roman times Welsh has clearly changed and developed and taken in new words first from Anglo-Saxon and then from Norman French, more recently from English. The miracle is, however, that despite conquest and occupation it has survived and today is daily gaining in vigour. Its survival it owes to two major factors – the bardic tradition that manifests itself today in the Royal National Eisteddfod and the natural defences of Wales herself, her forbidding hills and her inaccessible valleys. It is no accident that the areas where Welsh is most spoken tend also to be the most mountainous.

The great mountain stronghold of North Wales comprises 10 distinctive mountain groups: the Carnedds, the Glyders, Snowdon, the Eifionydds, and the Moelwyns north and west of the Conway and Festiniog valleys; the Rhinog and Arennig ranges east of Harlech; Cader Idris, the Arans and the Berwyns that form an outer rampart along the southern edge of the Dee – Dovey valley.

Beneath the stronghold lie old hard rocks – hardest and oldest of all in Anglesey and along the Menai Straits, a sort of geological buffer against which when the Earth was still molten immense pressures from the south built up the basic structure of the rest of Wales. The result is that all the valleys and their corresponding hills run roughly north-east, south-west. These pressures too, hardening the silts into slates, give us that most characteristic feature of the landscape of north and west Wales, the slate quarry. The mountains are of immense geological complexity. They are in fact only the ragged roots of much bigger mountains which were gouged and scoured during successive ice ages. Nowhere is the effect of the immense weight and power of the ice sheet more apparent than in the landscape round the Pass of Aberglaslyn south of Beddgelert and in the smoothing and flattening of Anglesey despite the hardness of its ancient rock. Volcanoes too have played their part in the formation of the quite spectacular landscape of the region. It would be wrong, however, to believe that any of the major peaks are old volcanoes in themselves as some people have claimed. Snowdon and the other mountains of the area have been carved out of a thick spread of rocks both sedimentary and

6

volcanic and these rocks have themselves been forced upwards to become high ground.

Geographers have put the frontier of North Wales along the Dee and the Severn but the area northwards of the Vale of Llangollen (the route of the A5) is merely the curtain walling of the real fortress. The name of this area – Clwyd – means gateway and the Clwyd hills which carry the northern end of Offa's Dyke – the ancient border – are as gentle as the sheep that graze their slopes. And the wide Vale of Clwyd is acknowledged to be more English in character than Welsh – as Daniel Defoe put it two hundred years ago '. . . a most pleasant, fruitful, populous and delicious vale . . . which made us think ourselves in England again all of a sudden.' Nor was the higher wilder dome of Denbigh with its massive afforested Mynydd Hiraethog a genuine barrier to the westward drive of English armies or English peoples. The real castle walls begin with the Carnedds, and the Conway is their moat.

The Carnedd mountains form the largest mass of high ground in Wales and are basically a ridge running north-north-east to south-south-west. In the north they begin with the impassable sea cliffs of Penmaenach behind Conway and end abruptly in a 2,000-foot drop to Llyn Ogwen at the head of the Nant Ffrancon Pass. On either side of the central massif steep ridges run out to make a mountainous area some 70 square miles in area and roughly square in shape. The two main peaks are Carnedd Llywelyn (3,485ft) and Carnedd Ddafydd (3,424ft) Tradition has it that Llywelyn ap Griffith, the last of the native Welsh princes, built a fortification on the summit of Carnedd Llywelyn during his struggles with Edward I, the eventual conqueror of Wales and one of the greatest castle builders of all times. The other commemorates Ddafydd, his brother.

Across the Nant Ffrancon Pass over which the A5 passes – once described as 'the most dreadful horse-path in Wales' – are the Glyders, a peaked and craggy contrast to the rounded grassy Carnedds. And the most peaked and craggy of all is the near-triangular Tryfan (pronounced Truv-Van) over 3,000ft high and only half a mile from the A5 highway. (See cover picture). Besides possessing a host of delights for the climber whether novice or expert, Tryfan has its own legend. Somewhere at its foot lies a cave in a rocky outcrop called Pen Bryn Melyn. A coach – the horse-drawn variety not the grockle-laden modern type – has been seen outside the entrance and it sets down a passenger who goes into the cave. Only one mortal ever followed him in and he found boundless riches there. The trouble was that next day he could find neither the cave nor the trail of pebbles he had laid. Besides Tryfan there are three other peaks in the Glyder range that exceed 3,000ft – the two Glyders, Fach and Fawr, form a ridge that runs west from Capel Curig parallelling the A4086 road, and Y Garn and Elidir Fawr form another running north-east from Tryfan. Between the two lies Twll Du (Black Hole) more commonly known as the Devil's Kitchen with a drop of nearly a thousand feet from the summit of Glyder Fawr on its eastern side. This huge and sombre cleft besides presenting rock climbers with a severe test of their physical and, some say, of their psychic powers, offers an open-cast view of what the geologists call the great 'Snowdon syncline'.

Between the Glyder range and the innermost stronghold of Snowdon lies the Pass of Llanberis and its long narrow double lake Llyn Padarn and Llyn Peris. Now the site – at Dinorwic – of one of the greatest slate quarries in the world, this rocky ravine long served as a *sanctum sanctorum* for those Welshmen who resisted alien rule. Llywelyn ap Iorwerth, Llywelyn the Great, Prince of Gwynedd, who held out against the English for nearly 40 years – he once captured Shrewsbury, in 1215 – had a castle at Dolbadarn, across the pass from Dinorwic. He kept his disaffected brother, Owen the Red, a prisoner there for 23 years. A later Welsh resistance leader, Owain Glyndwr, held the English Lord Grey of Ruthin prisoner in the same place in 1402 until a ransom of 10,000 marks was paid for him.

English sailors are reputed to have given the Snowdon range its name – seeing the hills covered with snow as they sailed along the coast, they named them 'Snowdunes' or 'Snawdun'. The Welsh name *'Eryri'* – the abode of Eagles – was used earlier but Llywelyn the Great adopted the title of Lord of Snowdon in 1230. Both titles then applied to all the mountains of this region of North Wales, the area we now call by the revived thirteenth century title of Snowdonia. Snowdon itself is the highest mountain range in Wales at 3,560ft and is a horsehoe of attendant peaks. The highest is Yr Wyddfa Fawr, on one side is Lliwedd, and on the other Crib Goch and Carnedd Ugain. (See page 84) Yr Wyddfa, the actual summit of Snowdon to most people, is the burial place of Rhita Fawr, a legendary Welsh giant who slew kings and wore a cloak woven from their beards – a cloak frequently visible to this day. Besides the peaks of the Snowdon range, the steep cwms between the mountains that make up the chain are themselves full of interest and legend. Cwmglas under Carnedd Ugain above the Llanberis Pass has a small and fishless lake, Llyn Cwmglas, which is supposed to hold hidden treasure in the form of the crown jewels of Ancient Britain hidden by Merlin after King Arthur's death. Cwm Tregalan, a bowl-shaped cwm flanked on the east by Lliwedd and on the west by Snowdon's south ridge, and the ridge which joins Lliwedd to the central peak, Bwlch-y-Saethau – the Pass of the Arrows – are, according to the Welsh version of the Arthurian legend, the true site of Arthur's last great battle with his traitor nephew, Modred. The story goes that Arthur was at Dinas Emrys by Llyn Dinas near Beddgelert when he heard of Modreds' betrayal to the Saxons. Modred and his supporters then held a fortified town, Treggalan, at the head of the rocky cwm of the same name close under Yr Wyddfa. Arthur marched his men over the wild country east of Yr Aran and took Modred in the rear. In the great struggle that followed Modred and his followers were forced backwards and upwards along the wide saddle of Bwlch-y-Saethau. At the moment of victory, Arthur was killed by a stray arrow and buried under a vast cairn of rocks at the head of the cwm. Later, it is said, this cairn was demolished to repair the famous Watkin Path that runs up from the lower cwm of Cwm-y-Llan. The story is certainly more credible than the English version that puts the site of the battle at an undiscovered locality called Camlann in that other Celtic stronghold, Cornwall. Not so credible is the follow-up legend that in the nineteenth century a shepherd stumbled into a cave on the east face of Lliwedd and found a vast concourse of Arthur's warriors asleep waiting for Arthur's promised return. The Watkin path, however, is real enough and was constructed in 1892 by Sir Edward Watkin. Here too a latter-day leader – W. E. Gladstone – climbed to a quite remarkable height up the cwm for a man in his eighties in order to make a speech to quarrymen. A rock bearing his name now marks the spot. The other cwm of especial interest is the northerly one of Cwmbrwynog which has the Snowdon Mountain Railway station at its head and contains the fearsome Clogwyn Du'r Arddu – the Black Precipice of Arddu – which was not climbed until 1927 but is now climbed regularly for the benefit of television.

Between the Snowdon range and the 'armpit of Wales' under the outstretched arm of the Lleyn peninsula – the sandy estuary of the rivers Glaslyn and Dwyryd called Traeth Bach – lies a small group of mountains in a triangular area called the Eifionydd. Their summits – eight in all and five of them above 2,000ft – make a distinct horsehoe shape, elongated with its open southward end on the road that runs from Tremadoc to Caernarfon. The principal height is Moel Hebog, 2,568ft. These are quiet, gentle hills and lonely pastures but there are one or two notable crags. One of these, a cliff on the flank of Moel-yr—Ogof, contains a cave – ogof – reputed to have been the hiding place of Owain Glyndwr, the Welsh national leader of the early fifteenth century who ransomed Lord Grey. Subsequently he was betrayed by his own countrymen who then helped King Henry IV's soldiers hunt Glyndwr all over Snowdonia. Eventually cornered near Aberglaslyn which, as its name indicates, stood in those days on the sea, Glyndwr swam across the estuary and found refuge in a cave in the face of a fearsome crag in the area of Cwm Meillionen.

The last group of mountains of the immediate Snowdon area, a sort of inner ward abutting the powerful central keep, are the Moelwyns. Moel means a bare, rounded hill and this is the general description of the range that runs, inevitably, NE-SW from the Dwyrwd estuary to the

Bettws-y-Coed – Capel Curig road. At the south-western end is the exception to the general description – Cnicht, a favourite with climbers which used to be known as the 'Welsh Matterhorn' because from some angles it has a tooth-like appearance. It is in fact a ridge half-a-mile long. The other Moelwyns are more characteristically shaped and the most easterly Moel Siabod (2,861ft), joined to the rest by a long col of bogs and heather, has been called the 'Elephant Mountain' because of its silhouette when seen from the east. From the highest of the southern summits – Moelwyn Mawr (2,527ft) – the view is said to be the best in Wales for variety, beauty and extent. The area is particularly rich in lakes and waterfalls. It is also an area of massive slate quarries although many of these have fallen into disuse. Above all this is the one area in Snowdonia where hill farming is practised in the traditional manner – Welsh Black cattle on the pastures in the valley floors, and lower, flatter slopes ; higher up, the *ffridd* – thin pasture bounded by stone walls where the sheep are wintered ; higher again the *mynydd*, the mountain itself where the sheep graze in all but the worst months of the year. And running precariously over mountainside, crag and peak the walls that mark boundaries and separate *ffridd* from *mynydd.*

Between the Ffestiniog valley and the Mawddach estuary with Barmouth at its upper lip, is a vast dome of ancient rock known to the geologists as the 'Harlech Dome' and to mountaineers as the Rhinog range. The rocks of the region are among the oldest in Wales and they lend to the Rhinogs a characteristically rugged angularity : flat tops rather than peaks, squares rather than triangles and smooth steep rock-walls. The area is also among the wettest in Wales and smooth wet cliffs do little for the rock-climbers. The name Rhinog is believed to be a corruption of the word *rhiniog* which means 'threshold' and, indeed, the Rhinogs could be seen as a sort of battlemented water-gatehouse to the central Welsh citadel to invaders from the sea. To carry the analogy further, there is a pass through the range called Bwlch Drws Ardudwy – 'the door of Ardudwy'. Ardudwy is at once the name of a coastal village as well as a hilly district of Merioneth. It has a claim on history on both counts. One legend is of a party of men from Ardudwy raiding the half-English Vale of Clwyd and carrying off a number of the women. The Clwyd men set off in pursuit and caught up with the raiders and their captives at Llyn-y-Morynion near Blaenau Ffestiniog. All the Ardudwy men were slain and to the astonishment of their rescuers all the Clwyd women promptly threw themselves in to the lake and were drowned. Since then the lake has had its present name which means 'The Maidens' – a name which surely must beg several interesting questions. Ardudwy's other claim to fame is that it was the birthplace of the Parliamentarian Colonel Jones, one of the more obnoxious of the regicides who married Cromwell's sister Catherine and was hanged, drawn and quartered in 1660. His remains lie in Llanenddwyn church.

The Arennig Range is in the area bounded in the west by the Mawddach river valley along which the A487 runs, the upper reaches of the Conway in the north, the valley of the Trweryn which flows into Lake Bala in the west and the Bala-Wnion valley which carries the A494, in the south. Arennig Fawr (2,800ft) with its double *moel* stands in the middle of a huge tract of deserted marsh and moorland. An unlucky Flying Fortress crew of the US Eighth Air Force 'found' it in the summer of 1943 and there is a memorial to them on the summit – these eastern peaks of the Snowdon range are littered with the wrecks of many wartime aircraft who suffered a similar fate.

On the other side of the Dee–Bala–Wnion valley lies a range of hills that amounts to outer parapet or rampart of the Snowdonian 'donjon'. It begins close to the coast in the west with the Cader Idris range, continuous beyond the Bwlch-y-Oeddrws and the Dinas Mawddy–Dolgellau road as the Arans and eventually ends above the Vale of Llangollen as the Berwyns. Although the Arans are slightly higher, the Cader Idris range is more distinctive because of its shape. It resembles a giant rocky wave just about to break, a sort of geological comber thrust up by some immense subterranean tide – an explanation perhaps with a grain of truth in it.

This great 'breaker' is six and a half miles from end to end, possibly the longest precipice in Britain. The highest top is Penygadair (2,927ft) with the hump of Mynedd Moel only a mile away to the east with Tyrau Mawr two miles to the west. The area is rich in legend but there is no basis for the often quoted translation that the name means 'Arthur's Seat'. There was a giant in Welsh mythology called Idris Gawr but there was also a real Idris, Prince of Merioneth, in the seventh century, who did heroic things against the Irish invader and he seems a more likely candidate to have a mountain of such magnificence named after him. Of more recent times, the mountain gave its name to a mineral water company which at one time owned a wood, now a nature reserve, on the shores of Tal-y-Llin.

The two main peaks of the Arans, Aran Fawddwy (2,970ft) and Aran Benllyn (2,901ft) are only about two miles apart and form part of the main ridge which runs parallel to the main Bala–Dolgellau road (A494). Although they are so close – indeed they might be mistaken for a single mountain – they actually sit astride the main north-south watershed of Wales. The waters of the southerly Aran Fawddy flow through the rivers Cywarch and Dovey down into Cardigan Bay whilst those of Benllyn flow northwards through the river Twrch to Lake Bala and on through the Dee to Liverpool Bay. By the same token, the countryside over which they preside is also different. To the south lies the high, close country around Dinas Mawddy and Mallwyd with its deep valleys and mountain passes and peaks, secretive and forbidding, even perilous to the stranger. To the north-east lie the soft hills of the Penllyn forest, the lake and the easy access to the Dee Valley. Hardly surprisingly, history has numerous examples of the men of those particular hills preying upon those in the lusher valleys beyond Bala, of the Welsh preying upon the English and of the English quite often carrying the battle back to the Welsh. Dinas Mawddy, in particular, was notorious from the sixteenth century onwards for the *Gwylliaid Cochion Maddwy* – the Red Brigands of Mawddy – who waged war on all comers and ranged far and wide on their expeditions of robbery, pillage and rape. Before they were finally suppresed during the reign of King Henry VIII they even waylaid and slaughtered one of the King's judges. How effective the measures were in the longer term is a matter of some doubt. Brigandage was rife in the area up to the time the roads were built and, as late as 1860, that inveterate Welsh walker, George Borrow, walked on quickly when he met red-haired men of villainous aspect around Mawddy. Indeed it is said that Mawddy people still show a prevalence of copper tones in their hair. Nonetheless, Mawddy today enjoys an unrivalled reputation for hospitality to visitors. Tourism makes good hosts of us all!

The Berwyns sprawl across the face of north-east Wales some 24 miles from the edge of the Penllyn Forest, south-east of Bala, to the Vale of Llangollen above Corwen. They are hardly mountains at all – by Welsh standards – although they average over 1,500ft over their length. Their highest peak is Moel Sych (2,713ft) and it is worth remembering once again that *Moel* means a rounded hill. The Berwyns are moorland hills with grass and sheep-farms on their lower slopes, moorland and grouse higher up. At their south-western end on the eastern slopes of Moel Sych some three and a half miles up the delightful Tanat valley from Llanrhaeadr-ym-Mochnant are the Pistyll Rhaeadr Falls, one of the seven wonders of Wales (see page 54). The name translated means 'Spout Waterfall' and indeed there are both to be seen: the first a near vertical fall of 120ft into a hidden basin; the second a 'spout' emerging from the outer rim of the basin. In the depths of the Berwyns is another enchantingly named village shown on the maps as Llanarmon D.C. – the D.C. standing for Dyffryn Ceiriog – 'Church of St Armon in the Vale of the River Ceiriog'.

At the eastern end of the range, the town of Corwen has associations with the fifteenth century Welsh hero we have met in several places earlier – Owain Glyndwr. He took his name from one of his estates at a places now called Glyndyfrdwy, four miles east of Corwen. The hills also have associations with other heroes – and heroines. 'Helen of the Legions' who gave her name to the Roman roads striking westwards through Wales – she was a native Welsh princess who married a Roman Emperor – lost all her provisions in Llyn Caws (Lake of Cheese) in the Berwyns. In these hills too, are a mass of cairns which bear Arthur's name as well as memorials to other Welsh gatherings to repel or assail the eternal enemy across Offa's Dyke, a mere three miles away.

Before we turn to a frontier of a different sort, it is worth considering Offa's Dyke itself – the ultimate curtain wall of the Welsh fortress but serving no defensive purpose other than demarcation. It is a remarkable earthwork that runs, with a few gaps, from the shore of the Dee in the north to the banks of the Severn near Chepstow in the south. It was built by Offa, a ruler of the Anglo-Saxon midland kingdom of Mercia in the eighth century and was at first defensive in character. In some places the ditch facing the Welsh side is 12ft deep and the bank some 60ft wide. It no longer follows the political boundary of Wales – over the centuries adjustments have been made in both directions – but it still has a time-honoured significance for all Welshmen. Going 'dros Glawdd Offa' is the equivalent of crossing the Rubicon – and burning one's boats. Offa's Dyke has come more into the public eye in recent times with the establishment of the Offa's Dyke Path. This runs 168 miles from Ffordlas near Prestatyn to Sedbury Cliffs overlooking the Severn Bridge.

The southern slopes of the Arans and the Berwyns, however, provide a different sort of frontier – one between Welsh kingdoms, Welsh landscape and Welsh people. The line is the effective transition from North Wales where the mountains tend to dominate the people to South Wales where the people tend to dominate the mountains. This is the border between the hard mountainous north and the softer, lusher south. Besides being the border of the old kingdoms of Gwynnedd and Clwydd in the north and Deheubarth (now Dafyd) and Powys in the south, it is also a dividing line of language and, to a lesser extent, culture. Words change subtly and with them ideas. More definitely it is something of a geological frontier. To the north lie all the old rocks that make up Snowdonia, to the south right to the Black Mountains and the Brecon Beacons the rocks are younger and softer and more easily weathered. In the analogy I have used so far, we have left the rugged inner keep of the Welsh castle and moved to the outer wards. They are still fortified but are no longer insurmountable. South of the Dovey the rocky turrets and mountain-filled skylines of the Snowdonia area give way to rounded peaks and boggy exposed moorlands of the Cambrian mountains. Running 30 miles from Plynlimon in the north to the rough hills of the upper Tywi valley above Llandovery, these thinly populated and rather isolated uplands were once called the 'Great Desert of Wales.' They did however provide a remote and unvisited refuge both for the Welsh nationalist cause – Glyndwr was proclaimed King of Wales in the delightful little town of Machynlleth in 1404 and held his first parliament there – and of the long-standing Christian tradition of Welsh culture. Strata Florida Abbey (Ystrad Fflur in Welsh, the Way of Flowers) a Cistercian foundation built at the end of the twelfth century, has been called the Westminster of Wales.

The Plynlimon range stands above an escarpment that rises suddenly to 2,000ft from a series of foothills running south from the Dovey valley. It probably takes its name from the Welsh for 'five beacons' – summits used in ancient times as sites from beacon fires in moments of danger. These five summits – Foel Fadian, Taren Bwlch Gwyn, Mawnog, Hengwm and the hill of Rhaeadr – run along the escarpment and dominate the whole area of the foothills towards the Dovey like a turretted curtain wall. The highest peak of the group is Pen Plynlimon Fawr (2,468ft) and is the source of one of the fastest flowing rivers in Britain, the Rheidol, and two of the longest, the Severn and the Wye. According to an old legend, the three rivers decided to have a race to the sea. The Rheidol chose the western side of Plynlimon, the other two the east. The Rheidol reached salt water three weeks before its rivals – which serves to demonstrate the nature of the Cumbrian mountains : steep to the west with plateaus and gentle slopes to the east. Afon Rheidol is full of magnificent wooded gorges where the tumbling river has bitten deep into the land in its haste to get to the sea. One such gorge forms part of the

Coed Rheidol National Nature Reserve and another, where the river turns sharply westwards and is joined by the river Mynach, is Devil's Bridge. Here the river passes through a deep gorge and is bridged by three bridges close together. Folk tales have it that the lowest bridge was built by the Devil when an old woman's cow was stranded across the gorge. Satan promised to build her a bridge if he could have as his own the first living creature to cross it. The woman agreed but when the bridge was ready she threw a piece of bread across and her dog chased it over. In fact the lowest bridge was almost certainly built by the monks from Strata Florida in the twelfth century. Then, however, the difference between the devil and a monk to a Welsh peasant was academic. The second bridge dates from the eighteenth century and the third from 1901.

The southern part of the Cambrian mountains is filled by rounded (*moel*) uplands broken by broad valleys. One of the most beautiful of these is the Afon Elan above Rhayader which was flooded to make four great reservoirs to serve Birmingham. This same region is also the source of two of the major Welsh rivers, the Teifi and the Tywy. The Teifi rises to the north-east of Tregaron near Strata Florida and flows through a vast peat bog, Cors-goch, some four square miles in area and the largest peat bog in Wales. The Teifi which is traditionally one of the best fishing rivers in Wales is once reputed to have had beavers. It flows on through Lampeter to the sea at Aberteifi better known by its English name of Cardigan. The river Towy rises on the slopes of Carn Gron and gives its name to a large area of forest — Forestry Commission plantations abound in this area — and runs into Llyn Brianne, now another reservoir. The Tywy then skirts round the foot of the Black Mountain through Llandvery, Llangadog and Llandeilo to Carmarthen and the sea. Both the Tywy and the Teifi have one feature in common — coracle fishers. At high tide in the salmon and sewin (a Welsh sea-trout) season the coracle men come with their black craft of ancient design upon their backs, the Teifi coracles being longer and slimmer than their Tywy counterparts.

Between the valleys of the Teifi and the Tywy behind St David's Head are the Preseli hills — called Mynedd Preseli in Welsh but hardly mountains in any real sense, a sort of hornwork to the Welsh bastion. The highest point of these rolling moorlands is only 1,760ft. Their interest lies in their stones for the whole area of Pembrokeshire has been described as a geologist's paradise and the Preseli Hills are the only possible British source of the dolerite bluestones of Stonehenge. There are 29 of them altogether some weighing as much as five tons and the question which has fascinated historians and geologists since the discovery was made in the early 1920s is how they came to be moved from Pembrokshire to Salisbury Plain in pre-mechanical, prehistoric times. The reason for their removal is perhaps more readily answered — the driving force of neolithic or Bronze Age religion that endowed the stones of this composition and character with a mystic significance. The Preseli Hills abound in stone circles, standing stones and megaliths or all types. One explanation is that the stones were carried on rollers to Milford Haven then by raft across the Bristol Channel and up the Bristol Avon and finally by rollers again to Stonehenge. Recent geological evidence suggests, however, that the transporting agent could have been the immense ice sheet that covered the area during the last Ice Age. Bluestones could have been carried by the ice eastwards and deposited somewhere in the Salisbury Plain area where they were found by the builders of Stonehenge. The question then to be answered is whether Stonehenge was holy because of the stones that were there or whether the spot was holy first and the stones came later.

The most impressive mountain range of South Wales, the Brecon or Brecknock Beacons follows the usual north-east — south-west line for a distance of just over 40 miles from the valley of the Tywy to Offa's Dyke — a sort of gatehouse and barbican to the Welsh fortress. In the west there is the Black Mountain then across the valley of the river Tawe, Fforest Fawr which runs eastward to the valleys of the Taff and the Tarell. Between there and the Usk valley are the Brecon Beacons proper and east-north-east towards the Wye and the border lie the

Mynedd Du – the Black Mountains. Finally, north of the Brecon Usk – the river here runs due east – is the domed upland of Mynned Epynt.

The Black Mountain has two high points – Fan Hir (2,460ft) and Fan Brycheiniog which is 200ft higher – the Carmarthen and the Brecon Fan respectively. Both have impressive layered cliffs carved out of old red sandstone and on either side of these tilted escarpments lie two small lakes – Llyn-y-Fan Fawr and Llyn-y-Fan Fach, the latter, enclosed at the foot of the encircling crest almost sheer 500ft above, has attracted to itself an aura of magic and has a legend of love between a shepherd and the lady of the lake. (See page 96) Their descendants were reputed to be great herbalists and healers and a book of some of their 'prescriptions' now lies in the British Museum. One begins – 'Take the tongue of a living frog . . .' But Llyn-y-Fan is now a reservoir and with so much magic and healing in its waters, the town of Llanelli which it serves should be an especially healthy and magical place to live in.

The road past the Cray reservoir – the A4067 from Sennybridge to Ystradgynlais – divides the Black Mountain from Fforest Fawr, formerly the great forest of Brecknock which was a royal hunting preserve during the Middle Ages. Along the valley of the river Tawe – the river which has Swansea at its mouth – there is also a change of rock type. The Old Red Sandstone gives way to softer limestone and one of the most remarkable cave complexes in the United Kingdom, the Dan-yr-Ogof. It begins at a major 'sink hole' at a place called Sink-y-Giedd at a height of 1,436 feet and emerges over two miles away 700ft lower. The caves were first discovered by the brothers Morgan in 1912 and contain a selection of stalactites, natural bridges, caverns and underground lakes. Part of the complex was opened to the public in 1964 but exploration still continues and new discoveries are reported every year.

The river Twrch runs into the Tawe near Ystradgylais and its name brings an echo of both hunting and the Arthurian legend. The murderous wild boar Twrch Trwth was hunted by Arthur and his men from Ireland into Dyfed, across Cardigan into this area where it finally escaped by swimming out to sea.

Brecon is the centre of the Brecon Beacons National Park which covers an area of 500 square miles. The actual 'Beacons' naturally take their name form their use for medieval signal fires – Wales was also a great place for signal fires during the Silver Jubilee celebrations – and their highest point is the distinctive shape of Pen-y-Fan, 2,906ft. The rock of these summits is hard again – Devonian Old Red Sandstone known as 'plateau-beds' – which gives the peaks a slabtopped profile. In many cases the softer rock of the lower slopes has been eroded to great hollows backed by precipitous faces. A particularly striking example is that of Corn-Du (Black Horn), a neighbouring peak of Pen-y-Fan. In the cwm below the crag there is a lake – Llyn Cwm Llwch – which legend says is the secret door to fairyland. Apparently it used to be opened to allow ordinary mortals to visit the fairies every May Day until one of the mortals stole a flower. Years later when the local inhabitants decided to drain the lake to collect the treasures of fairyland, a giant arose and threatened to drown Brecon and all the land around if he was ever disturbed again. At Llangorse Lake – Llyn Syfaddan – just east of Brecon, the threat of flooding became a reality, it is said, and a city can still be seen beneath the waters. (See page 100) The Brecon area also abounds in reminders of Imperial Rome – there is a Roman Fort at Y Gaer west of Brecon once excavated by the late Sir Mortimer Wheeler, Libanus now houses the superb Mountain Centre, and not far away is Sarn Helen, the Roman road that connected South Wales with the North.

North across the Usk valley from the Brecon Beacons lies the largely empty mass of sheep grazed heathland, Mynedd Epynt, its lush green lower slopes providing rich pasture for Welsh Black cattle and a host of horses and foals. South of the Brecons lies a completely different area : the 'Valleys', the powerhouse and industrial heart of Wales. It is also the most populated. Of the total population of Wales of about 2.75million, about 1.8million live in South Wales, almost 65 per cent of the people live in less than a quarter of the land area. And, moreover, 13 this development came very quickly. Only a century ago, the great series of valleys running down from the edge of the Brecon Beacons – the Rhonddas, the Ely, the Taff, the Rhymney, the Ebbw, and the Usk – still kept much of their natural peace and beauty. But the coming of the railways and the demand for the coal that is found in a 56-mile oval-shaped belt stretching some 16 miles wide from Carmarthen Bay to Pontypool produced the ravages of coal mining and an immense increase in population. The centre of this development is Merthyr Tydfil in the valley of the Taff. Its name is that of a martyred British saint, Tudful the daughter of the Lord of Brycheinog (Brecon), who died for her faith at the end of the Roman era. To many modern people, Merthyr Tydfil is the name for another form of martyrdom : exploitation, social degradation and political unrest. Times have changed, however, since the black days of the nineteenth century and as our pictures show (see page 108) the hills above the valleys are green again, the little terraced houses neat and colourful.

In the terms of castle architecture, a barbican was built as the outer defences of a gateway, sometimes on the far side of the moat. Two ranges of hills on the Welsh 'Marches' – the term derives from a Norman French word meaning border – might be described as being barbicans to the castle of Wales : the Black Mountains of Gwent, and the hills of Radnorshire, known as the Radnor Forest. Approaching the latter area along the traditional route from Leominster to Penybont and on to Aberystwyth (the A44) gives a particularly vivid impression of entering a gateway. One has hardly passed the sign proclaiming *'Croeso i Cymru'* ('Welcome to Wales') than the hills close in, wall-like, on either side. This is the Radnor Forest a mysterious rock dome consisting of several rolling hills – Black Mixen and Great Rhos are the highest, both over 2,000ft – and deep valleys called 'dingles'. It is a region of water – old, delightful spa towns like Llandrindod Wells, its water famous since the reign of Charles II – and waterfalls, one with the delightful name of 'Water-Break-its-Neck'.

The Black Mountains get their name because by some trick of the light they always appear to anyone approaching them from the Hereford plain as a long dark wall. They are in fact superbly coloured with purple heather topping their red sandstone flanks with green valleys beneath. The most splendid of these valleys is the densely wooded Ewyas along the banks of the Honddu stream and the only road on the eastern edge of the mountains. Here a celebrated monastery was built in 1188 by Hugh de Lacy, Earl of Hereford. (See page 88) Further up the valley are other ruins, those of the house built by the poet Walter Savage Landor, a contemporary of Wordsworth. Landor attempted to establish, like his other contemporary Thomas Johnes of Dafod, an 'earthly paradise' on his estate. His temperament – not for nothing was his middle name Savage – was against him and he abandoned the attempt and left to live abroad. He also left this epitaph to Llanthony which serves too to end this introduction to the wonders of Wales :

'Llanthony! An ungenial clime
And the broad wing of restless time
Have rudely swept thy mossy walls
And rocked thy abbots in their palls.
I loved thee by thy streams of yore,
By distant streams I love thee more;
For never is the heart so true
As bidding what we love adieu.'

Alan Hollingsworth
Bontddu, 1977

14

A Glossary of Welsh Place-Name Terms

Welsh place-names are usually made up by joining a number of word elements together. A vast number of place-names begin with *'Llan'* (Church) which merely serves to remind us that Wales was Christian when the greater part of the rest of Europe was pagan. Other words often encountered are *'aber'* (river mouth) *'llyn'* (a lake) and *'mynedd'* (a mountain). Other terms have the following meanings:

afon: river
bach or *fach:* small
ban: a high place
bedd: a grave
bont or *pont:* a bridge
bwlch: a pass
caer or *gaer:* a fort
capel: a chapel
carn, carnedd: a cairn
coed: a wood

coch or *goch:* red
cors: a bog or fen
craig: a rock or crag
cwm or *dyffryn:* a valley
Cymro: a Welshman
dinas: a fort or city
dol: a meadow
du: black
eglwys: a church
fawr or *mawr:* large

glan: ashore
glas: green
gwyn: white
llech: slate
maen: a boulder
moel: a rounded hill
nant: a stream
ogof: a cave
pen: a headland
pistyll: a waterfall
ystwyth: winding

(Thoughout this book we have been guided in the spelling by that in use on recent editions of Ordnance Survey maps.)

Tintern Abbey, Gwent — the jewel of the Wye valley. Founded as a Cistercian house by Walter de Clare in 1181, it became one of the wealthiest monastic foundations in the country. Most of the construction was carried out between 1269 and 1287 under Roger Bigod, Earl of Norfolk. The abbey was suppressed by Henry VIII in 1536 and has been roofless since its dissolution. The chief remains are the ruins of the magnificent cruciform church, the chapter house and the refectory. The nearby Abbey Inn is believed to have been the Abbey's watergate. The property was for many years in the hands of the Duke of Beaufort's family who presented it to the nation in 1900.

16

The Welshpool and Llanfair Railway near Heniarth station, Powys. Built with a 2ft 6in gauge track the W&L was opened in 1903 as, in effect, a branch line linking Welshpool with Llanfair Caereinon nine miles away. It became part of the Great Western but lost its passenger services in 1931. It was closed completely by British Rail in 1956 but reopened under the control of a preservation society in 1963 running from Llanfair to Sylfaen, three miles short of Welshpool. Its two original locomotives — built in 1902 — are 0-6-0Ts *The Earl* and *The Countess.* A later addition was a French-built 0-8-0T produced for German service on the Russian front during World War II. Other vehicles came from the Zillertalbahn in Austria and from the Sierra Leone Government Railway. The preservation society hopes to extend the line to Welshpool in 1980.

Tenby in Dyfed is one of the most attractive
holiday towns in Wales. Once a Norse
settlement, it became a Welsh stronghold
and was celebrated as Dinbych-y-pysgod
(Tenby of the Fishes). It was eventually
seized by the Normans who built a castle on
Castle Hill on the left of the picture. They
also fortified the town and on the landward
side the walls still stand. Each year St
Margaret's Fair (31 July) is opened by the
mayor and corporation walking in proces-
sion round them. Tenby was a bustling and
important port in the fifteenth and sixteenth
centuries and had connections with Bristol
and Cork and near the harbour there survives
a splendid example of a Tudor merchant's
house which is now open to the public.
Most of Tenby's attractive architecture,
however, dates back to the early nineteenth
century when it was converted by Sir
William Paxton into an elegant and popular
'watering-place'. As a Greek inscription in
Castle Square tells us : 'The sea washes away
all the ills of mankind'.

Tal-y-Llyn lake, Gwynedd, lies at the western foot of the Cader Idris range and is renowned for its trout fishing. The pass in the background is Llyn Bach and the road to Dolgellau can be seen rising steeply along its eastern slope.

22

Plas Gwynant on the south-east slopes of Snowdon is place of mystery and imagination in the mists and half-light. Near this place, legend has it, two dragons slept an immemorial sleep in a lake beneath a hill. One was white, representing the Saxons; the other red, representing the Welsh. The lake was drained and the dragons fought long and hard until at last the white was defeated and the red dragon triumphed to become the national symbol of Wales.

24

View from Snowdon on Llyn Nantlle Uchaf, Gwynedd. The Snowdon range has a necklace of lakes around it and this view from the summit — Yr Wyddfa — looks almost due west along the B4418 road to Nantlle and Penygroes. The small lake in the foreground is Llyn Dywarchen called the 'Lake of the Turf Island' because it still has a natural floating islet of twigs and turf on its surface whose existence has been recorded back as far as Middle Ages when it was much bigger. The area around Nantlle is famous for its slate quarries some of which rise sheer from the roadside to over 400 feet.

The Rhondda Valley — view over Blaenrhondda, Mid-Glamorgan. Despite the disfigure-
ment of the coal mines and their dumps, old
and new, there is a radiant beaury over the
valleys of South Wales. Blaenrhondda is at
the head of Rhondda Fawr — larger Rhondda
— famed for its great musical tradition established in the nineteenth century. The tradition continues through innumerable brass
and silver bands and the world-famous male
voice choirs of Treorchy and Pendyrus.
Until the 1930s there was no exit from this
end of the valley until unemployed miners
built a road across the upland moors.

28

A Welsh valley of a different sort – Ponter-wyd, Afon Rheidol, Dyfed. This is one of the most sparsely populated regions in Britain and its wooded slopes like those of the neighbouring rivers Aeron, Ystwyth, Leri, and Lynfant make it a magnificent bird sanc-tuary. Peregrines, golden plovers, kestrels and red grouse are all to be seen with the chance of a glimpse of the rare red kite now reduced to a mere 20 breeding pairs in the whole of Britain.

Also in Afon Rheidol — the Vale of Rheidol Railway which runs from Aberystwyth to Devil's Bridge and unlike the other narrow gauge railways with which Wales abounds it is owned and operated by British Rail. The line is worked by the last three steam locomotives in BR running stock, all 2-6-2Ts. The oldest is No 9 *Prince of Wales* which was built in 1902 when the line opened. The other two, Nos 7 *Owain Glyndwr* and 8 *Llywelyn* were built by the GWR in Swindon in 1923. The train climbs 650ft in its journey of 12 miles and the last four miles of the track run along a ledge carved out of the rock. At Devil's Bridge the train waits for approximately an hour to allow visitors time to see the Mynach Falls.

'Little Italy beyond Wales' – the village of Portmeirion, Gwynedd. Distinguished Welsh architect, Clough Williams-Ellis, a great fighter against the despoiling of the land-scape, set out to create a show-place village like Sorrento or Portofino. He chose a small rocky and wooded peninsula lying between the estuaries of the rivers Glaslyn and Dwyryd near Portmadoc in the armpit of Wales at the base of the Lleyn Peninsula. His intention was to provide a 'living' exhibition of the various architectural styles from 1610 onwards. Work began in 1926 and has continued ever since. The starting point was the early nineteenth century house on the water's edge which is now the celebrated Port Mereirion Hotel, a campanile (right centre) was added in 1928, the domed Pantheon (extreme right) came in 1958/9. Sir Clough – he was knighted in 1972 at the age of 89 – is also a collector of architectural relics of all kinds and refers to his collection as his 'Home for Fallen Buildings'. One example on the left of the picture is the colonnade from Arnos Court, Bristol. Within the village itself are six little shops selling Welsh handicrafts, honey and knitwear. One sells Portmeirion's own pottery – as attractive and colourful as the village itself.

34

Pembroke Castle is the largest and most impressive of the many Norman castles in Britain. On a superb natural site on a promontory in the Pembroke river, overlooking Milford Haven, this great castle, founded in 1097, was a key fortress in the settlement of Wales in the late eleventh century. A distinctive feature is the splendid round keep over 75ft high with a stone dome on top which was probably built by William Marshall, who was Earl of Pembroke from 1189 to 1219. Another feature is the gatehouse which has a complex barbican (outer gateway) and no fewer than three portcullises. In the adjoining tower Harri Tudur, the Welshman who became Henry VII and founded the Tudor dynasty, was born in 1457. During the Civil War the castle was attacked in turn by both Roundheads and Royalists as the sympathies of its occupants changed. It was finally subdued after repeated attempts to take it by storm on 11 July 1648 when Cromwell, present in person, sent for his heavy artillery. The unfortunate commander of the castle on that occasion, a former Parliamentarian, Colonel Poyer, was sentenced to death with two other renegades; they drew lots so that only one should die and the colonel lost. He was shot in Covent Garden.

The coast near Porthgain, Dyfed. This magnificent rocky coast about five miles east of St David's Head is at the heart of the Pembrokeshire Coast National Park and is accessible along the coastal footpath. In the autumn grey seal pups are born among the rocks on this shore.

38

40

Monnow Bridge, Monmouth, Gwent. The only Norman fortified bridge surviving in Britain and one of the few remaining in Europe, Monnow Bridge takes its name from the river Monnow (its Welsh name is Mynwy) which flows into the Wye and must be crossed to enter the town. The gatehouse was constructed in the thirteenth century as a toll-house and defence tower with a portcullis. Monmouth itself was the birth-place of Henry V in 1387 and another celebrated native was Geoffrey of Monmouth, the virtual creator of the great Arthurian legend.

Machynlleth is probably one of the most agreeable towns in Wales. Situated in the valley of the Dovey in Gwynedd, it lies at the base of a group of rounded hills and is a centre for the easier ascents of either the Cader Idris or Plynlimon ranges. Machynlleth was chosen by Owain Glyndwr to be the capital of the then 'free' Wales and he was crowned King of Wales there in 1404. His Parliament House, now extended and restored, is part of a building founded as a monument to Owain Glyndwr's memory and is open to the public. The distinctive clock tower dates from 1873 when it replaced the traditional Market Cross. Machynlleth is a centre for the sheep trade and for salmon fishing.

Gors Fawr – the stone circle near Mynach-log-ddu on the south-eastern flanks of the Mynydd Preseli range of hills in Pembroke-shire, Dyfed. Like Stonehenge in distant Wiltshire it served as a time-measuring device for religious purposes. Also like the inner ring of stones at Stonehenge it is composed of bluestones found only in the Preseli hills. Whilst it is easy to explain the presence of these large stones in Gors Fawr the reasons why the ancients felt is neces-sary to transport 80 or so similar stones to Salisbury Plain and how they achieved it remains an intriguing mystery. One explana-tion may be that this era was of particular religious significance well before Stone-henge was built. Certainly the hills remain rich in atmosphere and prehistoric relics.

Menai Straits — Telford's suspension bridge. Begun in 1818, work on the bridge, which carried Anglesey's only road to the mainland, was completed in 1826. It was the first suspension bridge to bear heavy traffic and is 1,000ft long; the roadway is 100ft above the water. The Menai Straits has a reputation for its fierce tides and from time to time schemes have been advanced to harness them for hydro-electric purposes. The Snowdon range is in the background to this picture.

Llanidloes — the Market Hall (Powys). Llanidloes is, to many visitors' surprise, on the Severn which rises high in the Hafren Forest on the slopes of Plynlimon about eight miles north-west of the town. The pleasant Market Hall was built in 1609 and the lower part provides an arcade for stalls and the upper part a number of council chambers.

Carreg Cennen Castle, — Llandeilo, Dyfed. Three things in Wales are eternally timeless — the hills, the castles and the legends and all three come together at Carreg Cennen Castle. Perched high upon a limestone crag, the castle overlooks the Black Mountain at the western end of the Brecon Beacons range (not to be confused with the Black Mountains to the east). The original castle was built, it is said, by one of King Arthur's knights, Sir Urien — yet another example of the pervasive Arthurian legend throughout the Celtic west of Britain. The present castle was built by a Welsh prince and was taken by the English in 1277. It was owned variously by John of Gaunt and Henry Bolingbroke and was demolished in 1462 to prevent its use by robbers. One of its more interesting features is a long narrow gallery running back into the hill for more than 150ft. At the end there is a wishing well . . .

Llanrwst Bridge, – River Conway, Gwynedd.
Carrying the date of 1636, the bridge across
the Conway at Llanrwst is said to have been
designed in part by Inigo Jones. The Conway
is one of the natural defences of north Wales
and until 1826 when Telford's bridge at
Conway itself was opened, this was the
major road bridge.

Pistyll Rhaeadr Falls near Llanrhaeadr-ym-Mochnant, – one of the seven wonders of Wales:

Pistyll Rhaeadr and Wrexham Steeple,
Snowdon's mountain without its people,
Overton yew trees and St Winefride's Wells,
Llangollen Bridge and Gresford Bells.

The village of Llanrhaeadr-ym-Mochnant – translated variously as 'the church by the falls of the swift brook' or 'the church by the brook of pigs' – is of interest to those who prize the Welsh tongue. It was here that William Morgan translated the Bible into Welsh about 1588 and gave the language the basis of its modern form.

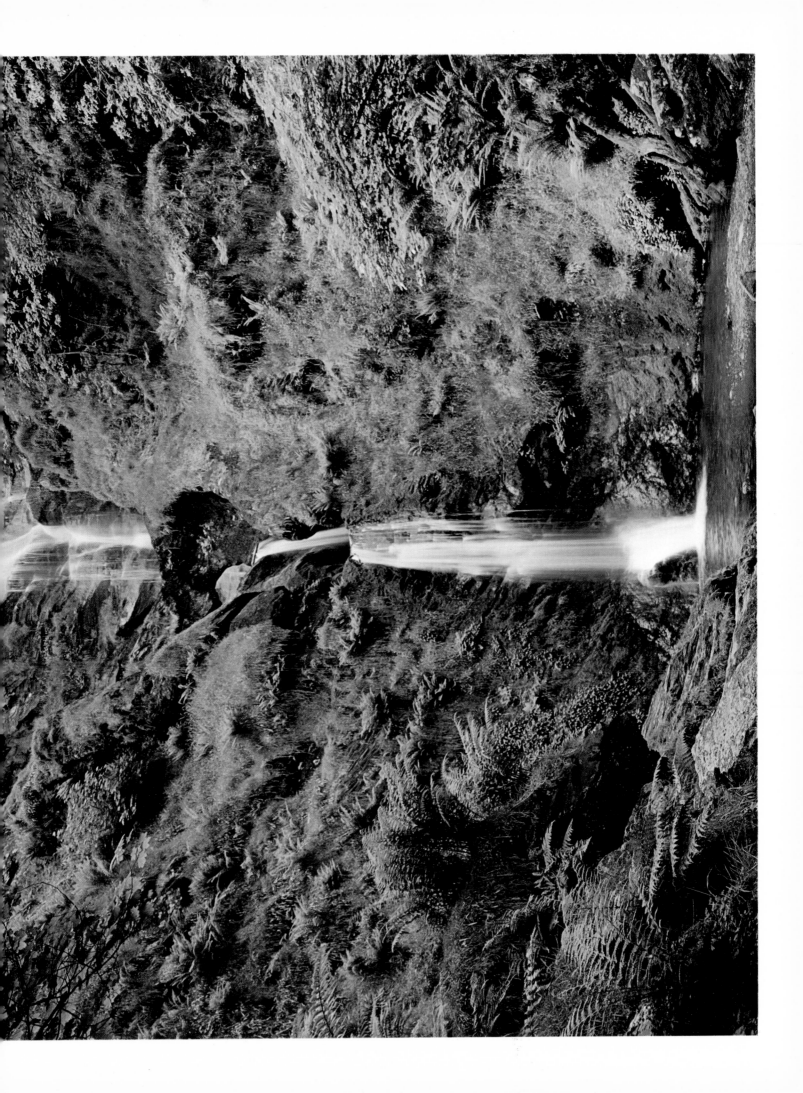

Britain's only rack-and-pinion railway – the Snowdon Mountain Railway which runs just over four miles and climbs to nearly 3,500ft between Llanberis and the summit of Snowdon. The train here is just beginning its climb up the first steep gradient across the Afon Hwch viaduct. Further up it climbs gradients of 1 in 5.5 and runs breathtakingly along the edge of the Clogwyn du'r Arddu precipice. The engines are steam driven and run on good Welsh coal mined in Glamorgan. The railway itself was opened in 1896 and was built to Continental standards and much of its equipment is Swiss.

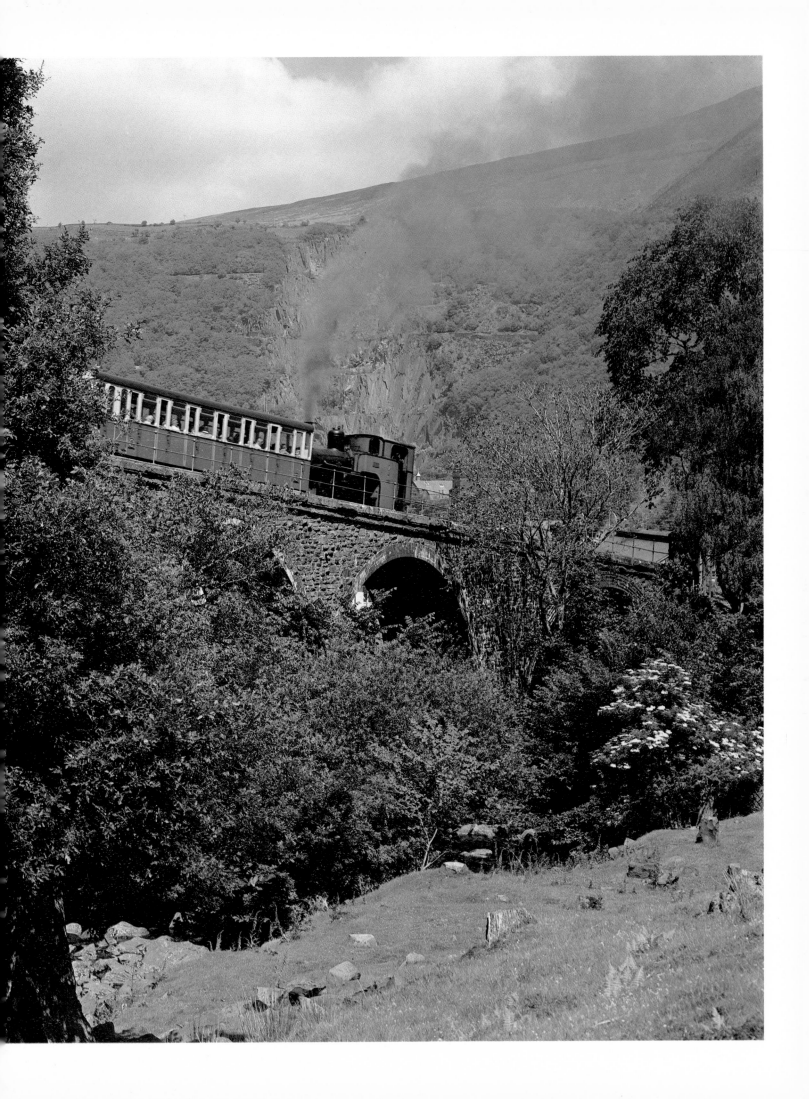

The Pontycysylltau viaduct across the River Dee at Acrefair near Llangollen in Clwyd. Carrying the Shropshire Union Canal, it was built by Telford between 1795 and 1805. It is 1,007ft in length and has 19 arches.

58

Nant Gwynant near Beddgelert, Gwynedd. The valley of the stream that runs from Llyn Gwynant into Llyn Dinas, Nant Gwynant separates the Snowdon range from the Moelwyns. On the right is a bluff on the rising slopes of Yr Aran (2,451ft). Nant Gwynant is the starting point of the Watkin Path to the summit of Yr Wyddfa. Beddgelert – the grave of Gelert – itself is the subject of some rather dubious Welsh folklore of eighteenth century origin. The tale of how Prince Llywelyn over-hastily slew his dog, Gelert, thinking from its bloody jaws that it had eaten his infant son when all the while the faithful beast had killed the wolf that would have eaten the boy, was the invention of an eighteenth century inn-keeper, David Prichard. Prichard was the first landlord of the Royal Goat Hotel at Beddgelert and thought up the legend, raising the stone that purports to mark the luckless animal's grave. As a heart rending Victorian poem – by W. R. Spencer – put it:

A pious monument I'll rear
In memory of the brave;
And passers-by will drop a tear
On faithful Gelert's grave.

In fact, if there is a grave in Beddgelert it is more likely to be under the local church and to be that of an ancient Welsh saint, Kelert rather than a faithful hound. Nonetheless, thousands of family parties visit the grave annually to this day. Even in 1798 it paid to publicise.

Mumbles Head, the Gower Peninsula in West Glamorgan. Situated at the eastward end of a cave-riddled stretch of limestone coastline, the twin islands of Mumbles Head guard the entrance to Swansea Bay. The lighthouse was built in 1794 when it was fully-manned and fortified. It is now automatic. The powerful ebb-tide knocks up a steep sea against westerly gales and there have been many shipwrecks on the Nixon sands which stand out from the point. As a popular poem of the Victorian era had it:

Mumbles is a funny place,
A church without a steeple,
Houses built of old ships wrecked,
And a most peculiar people.

The Mumbles — nowadays the definite article is inseparable from the name — is also a peculiar word. Some say it derives from the Welsh *Mynedd Moel* meaning bare mountain but the more attractive suggestion comes from Baedeker (c1906) who tells us that the name derives from the resemblance the rocks have to projecting breasts —
62 *mammae*, no less.

Carew Castle, Dyfed. Pronounced 'Carey', Carew castle is one of the most handsome ruins in south-west Wales sited on a lime-stone outcrop on the banks of the river Cleddau which flows into Milford Haven. Architecturally it is an excellent example of how Tudor landowners tried to open up castles as mansions. Carew had large mullioned windows, a great hall built in the fifteenth century, a fireplace in every major room and capacious cellerage. The recon-struction was carried out by Sir John Perrot, reputedly a natural son of Henry VIII. Like so many castles and fortified houses in the area, it was destroyed by the Parliamentarians at the end of the Civil War.

64

Cregennen Lake, Arthog, Gwynedd. Set 800ft up in the Cader Idris range are these enchanting mountain tarns under the beetling brows of Tyrau Mawr — 2,167ft. The Cader Idris range — the name means the abode of a mythical Welsh giant, Idris — is a great escarpment of old volcanic rock running ENE-WSW and overlooking the Mawddach estuary. Legend has it that anyone who sleeps a night on Cader Idris will wake either mad and blind or a poet.

St David's Cathedral, Dyfed. St David, the patron saint of Wales, founded a monastery at Glyn Rhosyn – Vale of Roses – the site of the cathedral, in 530AD. One of the legends told about him has it that when he and his followers first arrived, the area was terrorised by an Irish brigand called Boia. St David tamed him and, by all accounts, converted him to Christianity much to the fury of Boia's shrewish wife. To tempt the monks to break their vows of chastity she sent her servant girls naked to the monastery but St David's unflinching example, it is said, 'stiffened the monks' resistance'. The Cathedral itself is one of the great historic shrines of Christendom and the oldest cathedral settlement in the British Isles.

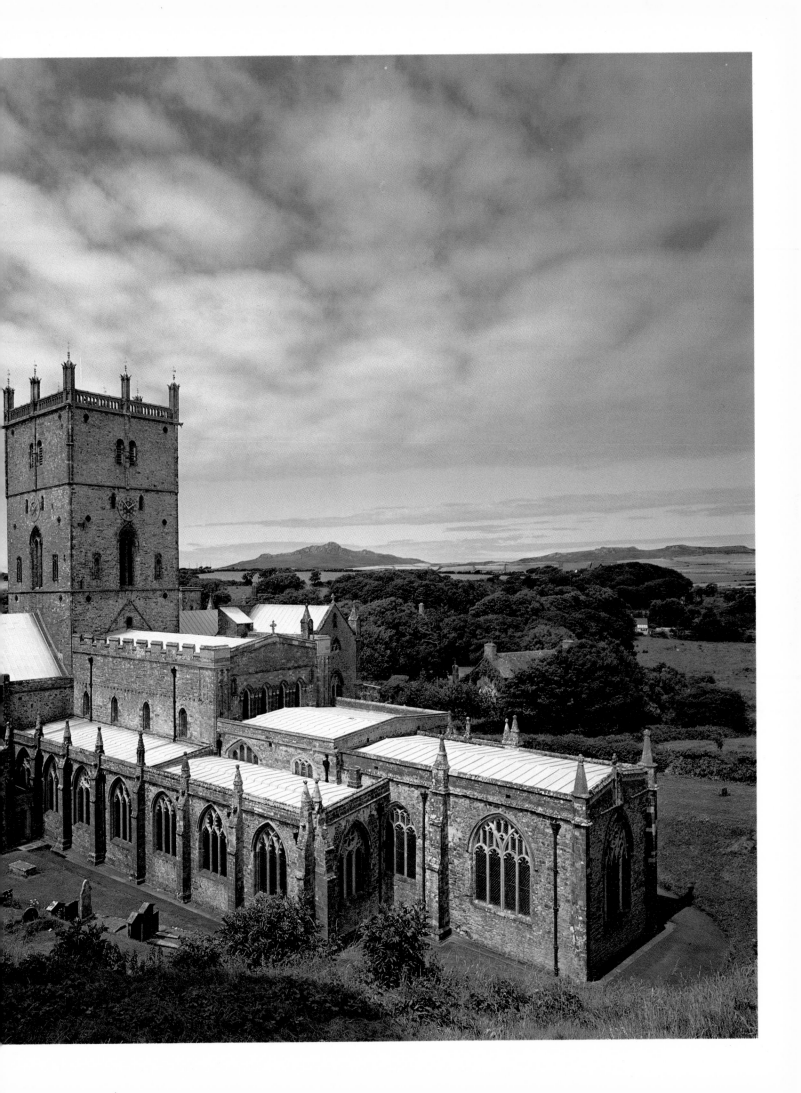

Sychant Pass, Penmaenmawr, Gwynedd. The old road from the delightful little town of Penmaenmawr which Gladstone thought so highly of, to Conway goes through the Sychant Pass and touches the village of Dwygyfylchi. The road rises over 300ft in a mile and then descends at a gradient of 1 : 7 with steep bends and precipitous drops.

70

Caernarfon, Gwynedd. The 'fort-opposite-Mona' and the ceremonial capital of Wales. It is situated on the Menai Strait at the mouth of the River Seiont, near the site of the Roman fortress of Segontium. Its majestic walls with their varying bands of coloured stone have been likened to the ancient walls of Constantinople. Some authorities suggest that Edward I chose the design to perpetuate the legend that the Emperor Constantine the Great, the first Christian Emperor of Rome, was born at Segontium. Edward I also began the tradition of proclaiming his eldest son as Prince of Wales at Caernarfon – a tradition repeated as recently as 1969 with the present Prince.

Tallyllyn Railway 0-4-0WT No 2 *Dolgoch* crosses the Dolgoch Viaduct with the Tywyn to Abergynolwyn train. Originally opened in 1866 for the carriage of slate from the quarries in the mountains to the coastal ports, the Tallyllyn runs for $7\frac{1}{2}$ miles. *Dolgoch* is one of the line's original locomotives and some of the original four wheel coaches also survive. Dolgoch itself — the name means 'red meadow or dale' — is noted for its rocky torrent and its magnificent rhododendrons.

The dam of Craig Goch reservoir, Powys. At the turn of the century the City of Birmingham purchased about 71 square miles of the Cwmdeudwr Hills near Rhayader including the valleys of the Elan and Claerwyn rivers, to build a reservoir. In the Elan valley — earlier renowned for its quiet beauty and where the poet Shelley once lived — engineers constructed a series of dams and flooded the valley behind them. The first of these was Craig Goch and was completed in 1907. It holds back a lake of 217 acres and is over 120ft high. The last of the series of dams — that across the Claerwyn was not completed until 1952.

76

Conway Castle, Gwynedd. The river Conway is one of the 'moats' of the Welsh fastness and the town and castle — Aberconwy, to give it its full name as it stands at the mouth of the river — were built on the orders of Edward I in 1283. Building of town and castle proceeded more or less simultaneously and by 1292 some £15,000 had been devoted to the task (about £5M in today's money). Most of the material was delivered by sea. The castle, which is still a remarkable well-preserved specimen of its type, suffered little during the Civil War when many other castles were devastated and this despite the fact that it withstood a Parliamentarian siege for three months. Most of the damage to its roof and windows occurred at the hands of the Earl of Conway who was given the castle by Charles II. The Earl dismantled all the lead, iron and timber and shipped it to Ireland but his ship sank on the way. Many saw this event at the time as fulfilling the 'Mermaid's Curse' that Conway — Lord or township — would always be poor.

The Estuary of the River Towy, Dyfed. The estuaries of the Taf, the Gwendraeths, and Towy rivers meet at Llanstephan south of Carmarthen to provide an attractive yacht harbour. Llanstephan village which nestles behind the castle on the peninsula is one of the best sited in South Wales. The castle, also superbly sited both pictorially – it was much painted by artists of the Romantic school of the early nineteenth century – and defensively. Its seaward facing slopes fall 150ft to the cliffs. Originally it was the site of an Iron Age fort and the present castle is believed to have been built about 1100 AD and rebuilt some 90 years later (c1192) by William de Canville. He is reputed to have borrowed the money from the Sheriff of Gloucester. The main feature of the castle still standing is the Great Gatehouse complete with chute for boiling oil and molten lead, and 'murder holes'. As the official guide book puts it, it was 'cruelly efficient'.

Bridge over the River Usk at Crickhowell, Gwent. This many-arched bridge presents an interesting optical illusion: from its eastern end all 13 of its arches can be seen, from the other end it appears to have only 12. The River Usk was once established — by Henry VIII — as the Welsh boundary, the area between the Usk and the Wye — once known as Monmouthshire — was attached to England. The division lasted for centuries until in 1974 the reform of local government returned Monmouth to Wales and restored its original name — Gwent.

The 'nails' of the Snowdon horseshoe from Capel Curig. The peaks are: Lliwedd, Yr Wyddfa (Snowdon summit), Crib Goch, Carnedd Ugain.

84

Chepstow Castle, Gwent. Following the Norman Conquest, William FitzOsbern was created Earl of Hereford and he built Chepstow Castle on a spectacular site on the top of limestone cliffs overlooking the Wye. He then used it as a base for his advances into the Welsh kingdom of Gwent. Because of its strategic importance the castle had a keep built of stone instead of the more usual timber and FitzOsbern's 'Great Tower' survives to this day. It has been altered over the years but the masonry of the cellar and the two lower storeys date back to the original construction between 1067 and 1072. The castle was the centre of fierce fighting during the English Civil War in 1645 and was taken by Parliament in 1648. It was spared from the demolition which was the fate of many Welsh castles of the period because of its usefulness as an arms store and as a prison notably for the Royalist bishop, Jeremy Taylor. The Royalists had their revenge, however, at the Restoration when Henry Marten, one of the regicides, was imprisoned for 20 years in the tower which stands on the left of the gatehouse. It is still known as Marten's Tower.

Llanthony Priory, Black Mountains, Powys. 'A place truly fitted for contemplation, a happy and delightfull spot' — thus wrote Geraldus Cambriensis the chronicler of Welsh life in the twelfth century. The monks of the day hardly shared his opinion. They are on record as asking: 'Who wants to sing to the wolves?' It was, however, the very serenity of the location that led to the setting up first of a hermitage during the reign of William Rufus and later to the establishment of the Priory. It was dissolved by Henry VIII in 1536 and fell into ruin. Although an attempt was made to re-establish the foundation in the nineteenth century, it was unsuccessful largely because the instigator, Walter Savage Landor, a friend of Browning and Swinburne, could not adjust to the neighbourhood. As a poet he too may have thought his song wasted on the wolves.

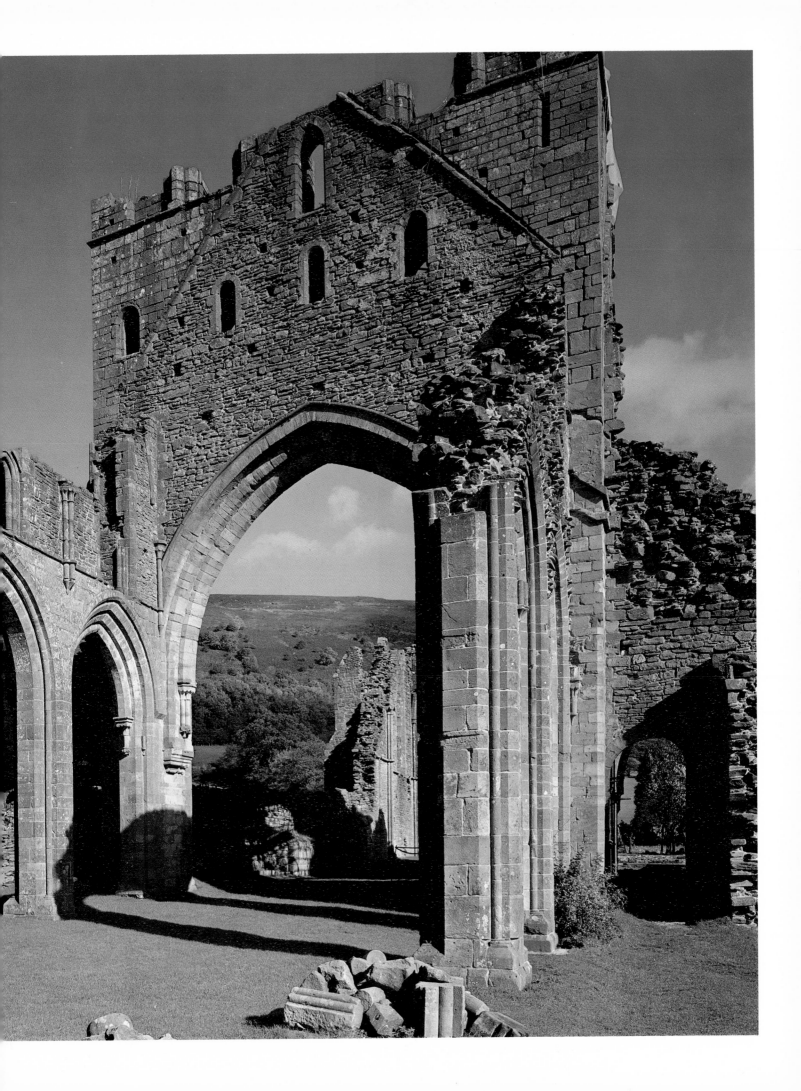

Brecon Beacons from the Mountain Centre, Libanus, near Brecon, Powys. The mountains take their name from their use in earlier times as the site of signal fires. The highest peak is Pen-y-Fan which reaches 2,906ft. It is the highest mountain in Britain south of Cader Idris and in clear weather the view from its summit includes the Cader Idris range to the north west, the Bristol Channel and the hills of Somerset and Devon, the Malvern Hills. Although the Brecon Beacons are not as rugged and challenging to the hill-walker as the mountain heart of Wales in Snodownia, and are mostly covered with springy turf, they have claimed many victims in their time. None perhaps is more tragic than poor Tommy Jones who was lost in 1900 on the way to his grandfather's farm between Brecon and Pen-y-Fan. His body was not found for nearly a month. There is now a memorial on the flanks of Pen-y-Fan which bears the boy's name.

90

Bosherton Cliffs, St Govan's Head, Pembroke, Dyfed. In this area, the carboniferous limestone and the Old Red Sandstone coincide to give another Devon beyond Wales. The fields are red and the sea-torn cliffs are made of stacks of limestone blocks frequently cut away into deep crevices and caves. St Govan has his (or her's) tiny chapel jammed half way down a typical ravine. Some people believe that St Govan was the Arthurian knight, Sir Gawain, others that the saint was the wife of a local king, Queen Cofen.

Blaenau Ffestiniog, Gwynedd. Slate has been quarried in North Wales for more than two centuries and an immense vein of slate runs right through the Glyder–Elidir range of mountains. At some places the slate can be quarried on the surface – Penrhyn is the best example – but at Blaenau Ffestiniog it was necessary to burrow underground and there are many miles of subterranean passages and chambers in the hills surrounding the town. One such chamber, in the Oakeley Quarry of Ffestiniog, is said to be big enough to contain St Paul's Cathedral. But for many thousands of people in all walks of life throughout Britain, Blaenau Ffestiniog represents an outstanding achievement in the creation and development of the narrow gauge amateur-run railway. The line was closed when the slate business declined after the end of World War II and in 1954 an impecunious group of enthusiasts was formed to take it over. Over the years thousands of men have given time and money to shift rock and rubble and help maintain rolling stock and stations. The last section of the line was drowned under a reservoir and a new section is now being built to replace it – a feat that has meant moving mountains both physically on the site and metaphorically in the courts and against the bureaucrats. The Ffestiniog Line is now the major project of its kind in the United Kingdom and an inspiration to many others all over the world. It is a major attraction to visitors and annually

carries over 200,000 passengers.

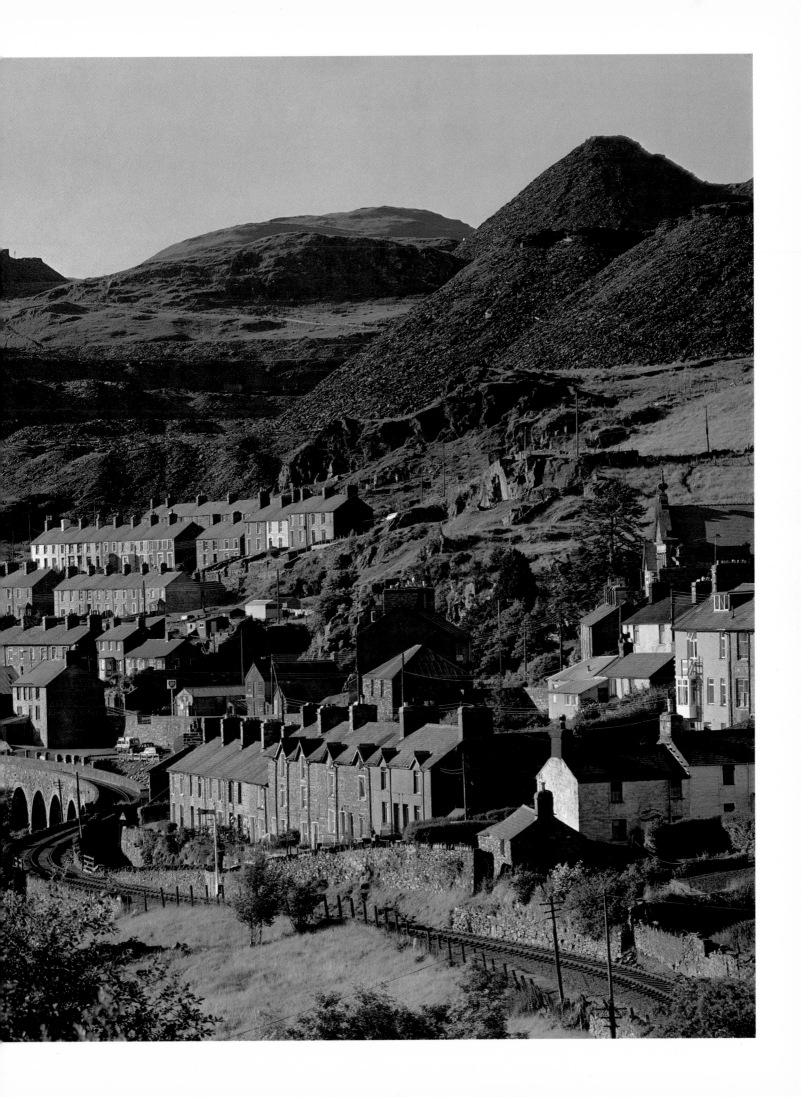

The Black Mountain — the Sawdde stream near Llyn-y-Fan-Fach. Whilst the bulk of the Brecon area is red in aspect the wild rocks of the Black Mountain at the western end of the range have a darker more menacing hue although the Mountain takes its name from a dark peat bog at its crest. It has two high points — Carmarthen Fan (2,460ft) and Brecon Fan (2,660ft) — with two small lakes, one on either side. From these lakes — Llyn-y-Fan-Fach and Llyn-y-Fan-Fawr — the river Sawdde runs north west to join the Towy near Llangadog. The smaller of the lakes and the most difficult of access, Fan Fach, has a celebrated legend. A lake fairy married a local farmer about 750 years ago and bore him three sons to whom she taught the secret skills of using herbs to cure all ills. The fairy eventually left the farmer and went back to her lake but returned from time to time to continue the instruction of her sons. They in turn passed on their skills from generation to generation until the last descendant, famous as a healer, died in the nineteenth century.

The other Black Mountains — at the eastern end of the Brecon Beacons National Park. This is the view from Gospel Pass over Hay-on-Wye. The road from Hay-on-Wye south to Llanthony Priory (see page 88) and the former monastery at Capel-y-ffyn — later the home of Eric Gill the sculptor and typographer — was much trodden in earlier times by monks and other clerics — hence its name. It passes along the valley of the river Honddu and between the twin hills of Lord Hereford's Knob (2,263ft) on the left and Hays Bluff (2,220ft) on the right.

Sunset over Llangorse Lake, Powys. Called *Llyn Synfaddan* in Welsh, this is the largest natural lake in South Wales. Behind it on the skyline is the distinctive shape of Pen-y-Fan and the Brecon Beacons. On the far side of the lake is the church of Llangasty – Tal-y-Llyn with the Gader Hill overshadowing it – recalling another, better-known Tal-y-Llyn and a greater Cader (Idris) further north. The lake itself was renowned in the middle ages for its eels – it is still prolific in coarse fish of all types – which gave rise to the Welsh expression *'cyhyd a llyswen Syfaddan'* ('as long as a Syfaddan eel'). Inevitably, too, there is a legend associated with the lake. It seems that once all the land around was owned by a cruel and greedy princess who agreed to marry her lover provided he brought her wealth. He promptly killed and robbed a rich merchant and gained his princess but also the curse of the dying merchant to the effect that the crime would be avenged on the ninth generation of their offspring. Over generations a city was built and prospered until one night a terrible flood burst from the hills and drowned it and all its inhabitants. It is said that the city can still be glimpsed under the water of the lake and that its church bells can also be heard. Its fate, no doubt, accounts too for the size of the eels.

Landscape near Blaen-y-Cwm, Dafyd. This cwm is in the upper reaches of the Ystwyth valley on the Hafod estate now owned by the Forestry Commission. About 180 years ago it was one of the most celebrated places in Wales and was visited by a host of travellers. Here Thomas Johnes (1748-1816) sought to improve the amenities of a ruined estate he had acquired by building upon it an 'Earthly Paradise'. He built a romantic country mansion with the advice of Baldwin and, later, Nash which was of Italianate appearance and was domed. As the poet Coleridge visited Hafod it is assumed that he had it in mind when he wrote of Kubla Khan and his stately pleasure-dome. But Johnes did more than build for his own comfort. He planted acres of ornamental trees, built roads and bridges and good cottages for his estate workers. The house was burned down in 1807, partially rebuilt until family tragedy forced Johnes to abandon it in 1811. It crumbled and became a ruin until it was finally blown up in 1950. Its site is now that of a caravan club.

Aberystwyth, Dyfed. 'The mouth of a twisting river' – Aberystwyth is sometimes called the 'Brighton of Wales'. In addition to its attractions as a seaside resort in the Georgian tradition, it is also the site of the National Library of Wales and of the University of Wales. On the left of the picture is the ruined keep of the Norman castle built during the reign of Edward I which played an important role in his conquest of Wales. It was completed in 1279 but its construction was criticised by its first governor who complained to the King that the foundations of the castle were too near the shore and that it was 'shaken day-in and day-out by the great crash of waves'. These same great waves are also popularly assumed to have been responsible for the establishment of the local lobster-fishing industry when a giant lobster was thrown by a huge wave over the roof tops into the High street. Until then nobody knew there were lobsters in Cardigan Bay – or so it is said but then, Wales is the country of myth and mellowed truthfulness.

Torpantau Waterfall, Blaen-y-Glyn. A typical valley of the afforested slopes of the Brecon Beacon range. These mountains are topped with a type of Old Red Sandstone rock known as 'plateau beds' which gives them their flat-topped appearance.

The Little Rhondda Valley, Tylerstown, Mid-Glamorgan. There are very few coalmines in evidence in the Rhondda valleys nowadays — a total of three compared with 50 in 1930 — but the legacy of its hey-day is still evident not least in the rows and rows of terraced houses that seem to fill it. No longer the homes of miners who walked to the pithead, these houses, substantially stone-built and now modernised and re-decorated in bright colours instead of the all-pervading grey, are much in demand by workers who commute to such places as Pontypridd, Cardiff and Llantrisant. There is a daily outflow from the Rhonddas of almost 30% of the population.

Bala Lake near Pentre – Piod, Gwynedd. *Llyn Tegid* – the real name for the lake near Bala – is the largest natural lake in Wales, 4½ miles long and a mile wide. It offers excellent fishing but its celebrated mystery fish – the gwyniad, a white scaled salmon – is seldom taken by line. Bala has the usual crop of legends that surround lakes in Wales. One says there is a palace beneath its waters, another that it has flooded the town of Bala once and will do again, a third that the Dee flows through the lake without their waters mixing. The cattle, incidentally, are Welsh Blacks.

110